745.5
DEV

Devonshire, Hilary.

Greeting cards and
gift wrap.

$17.71

33197000019997

DATE			
4-6			
4-14			
2-12			
7-3			
	DISCARDED		

BAKER & TAYLOR BOOKS

GREETING CARDS AND GIFT WRAP

Hilary Devonshire

Consultant: Henry Pluckrose

Photography: Chris Fairclough

FRANKLIN WATTS
New York/London/Toronto/Sydney

Copyright © 1992 Franklin Watts

Franklin Watts, Inc.
95 Madison Avenue
New York, NY 10016

Library of Congress Cataloging-in-Publication Data

Devonshire, Hilary.
    Greeting cards and gift wrap/by Hilary Devonshire.
        p. cm.—(Fresh start)
    Summary: Presents step-by-step instructions for decorating paper
using various techniques such as stenciling, printing, and marbling;
and demonstrates how to make special occasion cards and wrap gifts
creatively.
    ISBN 0-531-14219-1
    1. Paper work—Juvenile literature.   2. Greeting cards—Juvenile
literature.   3. Gift wrapping–Juvenile literature.   [1. Paper
work.   2. Handicraft.]   I. Title.   II. Series: Fresh start.
TT870.D42 1992
745.594′ 1-dc20   91-39594
                                                                     CIP AC

Design: Edward Kinsey

Editor: Jenny Wood

Typeset by Lineage Ltd,
Watford, England

Printed in Belgium

Contents

This book describes activities which use the following:

Adhesives – cold-water paste
– glue (UHU glue sticks, Bostick Solvent-Free, Copydex))
– adhesive pads

Assorted objects for printing (old kitchen utensils, corks, thread spools, garden sticks, junk pieces)

Brushes – flat-headed brush for stenciling
– old brushes (washing-up brush, nailbrush, toothbrush)
– wide brush

Carbon paper

Cardboard (thin white cardboard and scraps of thick cardboard)

Cardboard box (large)

Containers (small bowls or dishes, jelly jars, old ice-cream cartons)

Craft knife

Diffuser spray

Dishwashing liquid

Dyes – cold-water dyes

Fork (old)

Glitter

Hole punch

Inks – drawing inks
– marbling inks
– printing inks, water-based

Leaves

Linseed oil (boiled)

Newspapers (separated sheets)

Paints – acrylic paints
– poster or powder paints
– water color paints

Paper – good quality typing paper
– construction paper
– white and colored backing paper

Paper napkins (or paper towels) (plain, white)

Pencil

Pens (felt-tip, gold and silver)

Printing roller

Printing sheet (or tile), (plastic)

Ribbon (or string or thread, for gift tag ties)

Ruler – metal, for use with craft knife
– wooden or plastic

Scissors

Screen printing frame and squeegee

Sponges (thin, flat)

Spoons (old)

Sugar

Tray (deep, for marbling)

Vinegar

Water

There are many different ways of producing decorated papers. With methods such as printing or stenciling, the basic design can be repeated many times. But with methods such as marbling, the pattern is captured only once and therefore has its own unique charm.

Much pleasure can be gained from successfully producing homemade papers, and they can be used for many purposes. Presents for friends and relatives can be wrapped in your own decorated papers and accompanied by a matching card or gift tag. Some ideas for cards and gift tags are included in the following pages.

As you work, you will discover how different materials behave, how thickly or thinly to use the paints, which are the most suitable inks or papers, and which tools are best. You will learn these things only by experimenting for yourself. Try to use the different techniques described in this book to develop new designs of your own. Turning an idea into something new is being truly creative. Have fun!

1 Some of the equipment and materials you will need when making the decorated papers and cards described in this book.

Paste and paint papers

Using a colored paste mix is an easy way of making colorful papers. Once you have covered your paper with a layer of color, you can use all kinds of objects to create interesting patterns and designs.

You will need wallpaper paste, water, two mixing bowls or old ice-cream cartons, a spoon, paints, a teaspoonful of dishwashing liquid, a stick for stirring, sheets of newspaper, paper, a wide brush, and assorted objects with which to make a print.

1 Prepare some wallpaper paste, mixing until you achieve a creamy consistency. In a separate bowl, mix together some paint, the dishwashing liquid, and a small amount of the ready-mixed wallpaper paste. Stir until smooth.

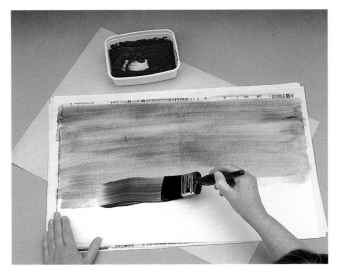

2 Arrange the sheets of newspaper into a pile, and place a sheet of paper on top. (The newspaper gives a soft surface for painting, and you can easily remove the top sheet if it becomes too sticky with paste.) Use long, quick strokes to brush the colored paste across the paper. Work first in one direction ...

3 . . . then in the other direction.

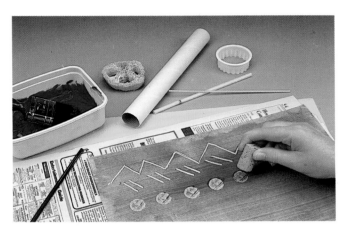

4 While the paste is still wet, use a piece of stick to scratch out a design, or press an object down onto the paste, then lift it away. The object will leave an impression of its shape. Here a cork is being used to create a design.

5 Here a pastry cutter is pressed into the paste, twisted . . .

6 . . . and lifted away. A thread spool is then pressed into the center of each shape, to create an interesting pattern.

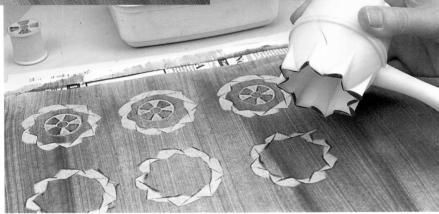

7 The finished design.

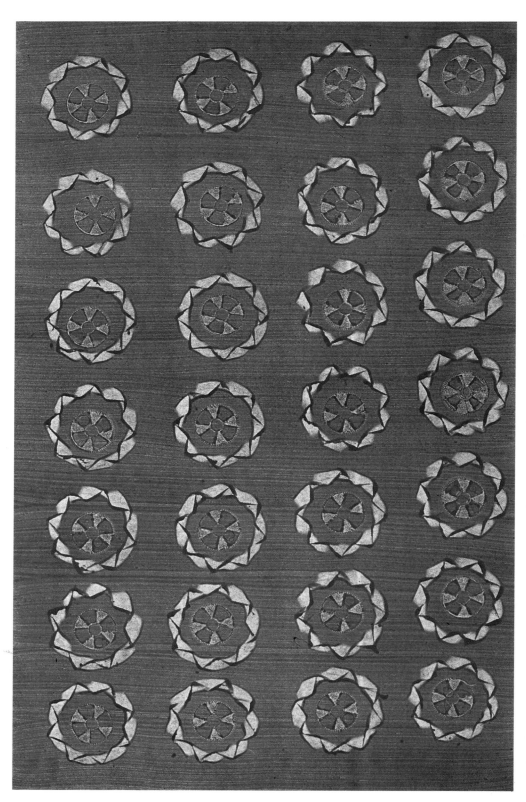

8 A selection of paste and paint papers.

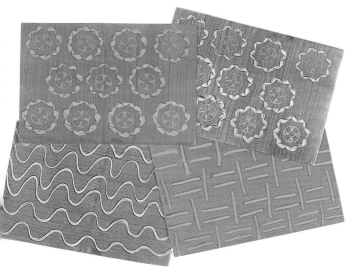

9 Instead of covering your sheet of paper with a wash of colored paste, leave the paper white. Press your printing object (for example, the thread spool or pastry cutter) into the colored paste mix, then make a colored pattern on the white paper.

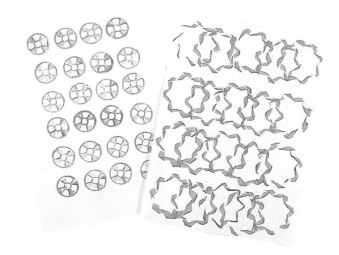

10 Use your decorated paper to wrap a gift and make a matching card.

Vinegar and sugar paste papers

Working with vinegar and sugar paste will give an unusual shine and texture to your finished designs.

You will need a mixture of malt vinegar and sugar (one part vinegar to two parts sugar), a jar (with a screw top), a spoon, a bowl or old ice-cream carton, water-color paints, an old fork, sheets of newspaper, paper, a wide brush, and pieces of thick cardboard.

1 Put the sugar and vinegar into the jar.

2 Screw the top of the jar on tightly, then shake the jar until the sugar and vinegar are well mixed.

3 Pour the mixture into the bowl and add a little paint. Whisk well with the fork to make a paste.

4 Arrange the sheets of newspaper into a pile, and place a sheet of paper on top. Brush the vinegar and sugar paste across the paper. Notice how the bubbles leave an interesting pattern. Leave the paper for about five minutes to allow the paste to set slightly.

5 Draw a pattern in the paste with a small piece of thick cardboard or with a cardboard comb (a piece of cardboard with notches cut into one end).

6 Papers patterned using vinegar and sugar paste.

7 If you add more sugar to your paste mix, the designs, when dry, will have a shinier finish.

8 Another idea for a
vinegar and sugar
paste design.

Roller-patterned papers

Another method of making patterned paper is to apply color with a printing roller.

You will need a plastic sheet, acrylic paints, a printing roller, and paper.

1 Put a little color onto the plastic sheet. Dip the roller in color and roll it across the paper. Use several colors for your pattern.

2 A colorful rollered paper.

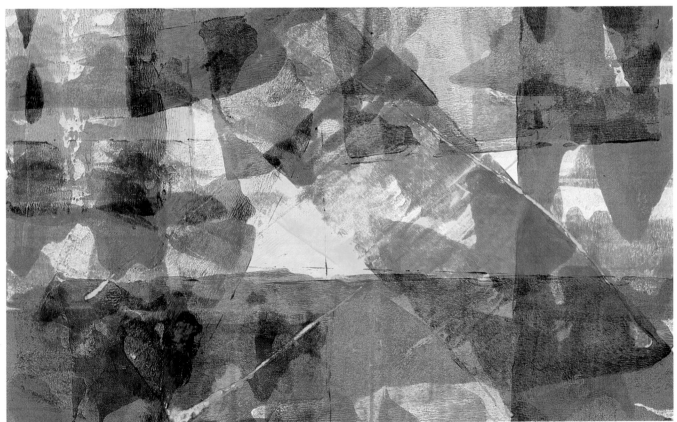

A greeting card

To make this card you will need thin white cardboard, a pencil, a craft knife, a metal ruler, scissors, a sheet of roller-patterned paper, and glue.

3 Cut a square window in the center of a postcard-sized piece of cardboard. Use this as a frame to help you select an interesting section of patterned paper. Using the inside edges of the frame as guidelines, draw around the edges of the patterned square you have chosen.

4 Fold another piece of cardboard in half to make a basic greeting card shape. Mark and cut out a square window in the front of the greeting card. The window should be the same size as the square on the patterned paper. Cut out the patterned square leaving a ½ inch border around the edges. Glue around this border (on the patterned side of the paper). Stick the patterned square onto the window of the greeting card so that the pattern shows through and becomes the picture on the front of the card.

5 The finished card accompanies a package wrapped in the rest of the roller-patterned paper. Notice the matching gift tag on the package, too. Your gift tag can be made from a folded or unfolded piece of cardboard. Punch a hole at one end for the tie.

Stenciled patterns and pictures are created by applying color to a stencil sheet from which a design has been cut. When the sheet is removed, the colored stencil print remains.

You will need pieces of sponge, boiled linseed oil, thin white cardboard, a pencil, paper, carbon paper, a craft knife, a metal ruler, a flat-headed brush, paints, adhesive pads, felt-tip pens, and scissors.

Making a stencil sheet

1 Using a piece of sponge, apply a little linseed oil to the surface of a sheet of white cardboard. As the oil is absorbed, the cardboard will become translucent. Set aside to dry.

A bird stencil

2 Draw a picture on a sheet of paper. Keep the shape of your picture fairly simple, with strong, clear lines.

3 Place a sheet of carbon paper (carbon side down) over the oiled stencil sheet. Now place your picture on top. Draw over the lines of your picture carefully and firmly. The carbon will transfer the lines to the stencil sheet.

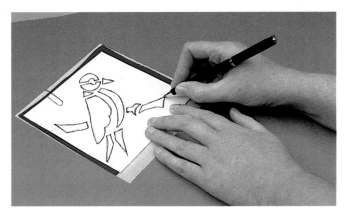

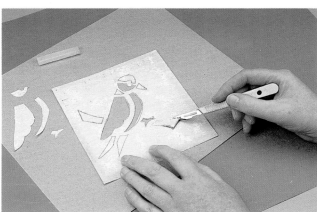

4 Using the craft knife, carefully cut around the outline of the design as it appears on the stencil sheet.

Leave some cardboard "bridges" between the sections, to strengthen the design.

5 Place the stencil on a sheet of paper. Using the flat-headed brush and only a little color, dab paint through the stencil.

6 A repeat pattern can be made. Remember to wipe the stencil sheet clean before repeating a stencil, or before changing the color.

Making a 3-D card

7 Cut out one of your stenciled pictures and attach two adhesive pads to the back.

8 Make a basic greeting card shape from a piece of cardboard. Glue a piece of colored paper onto the front of the card, if you wish, for added effect. Press the cutout stenciled picture onto the front of the card. The adhesive pads raise the picture above the surface of the card, to give a 3-D effect.

9 Use felt-tip pens to add some more decorations to your design.

10 The finished card.

A folded symmetrical design

11 Cut a square from thin white cardboard, fold it three times as shown, and cut small pieces from the folded edges.

12 Carefully unfold the cut square to reveal the symmetrical pattern.

13 Use a piece of sponge to dab color onto your stencil. Use very little paint so that it does not run under the edges of the stencil.

14 The sponge gives a soft, mottled effect.

15 A repeat symmetrical pattern.

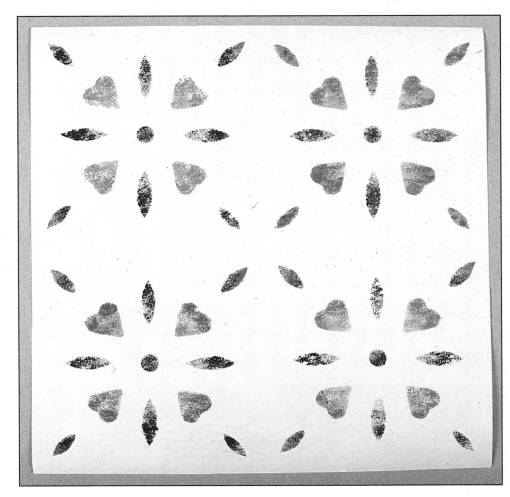

In this method of paper decoration, the outlines of shapes are shown by splattering paint around their edges. This creates a "negative" image in which the shapes remain uncolored. Compare this to the "positive" images formed by the stenciling process (see pages 17-23), where the design itself is colored.

You will need a large cardboard box, paper, some leaves, paints, an old brush, and a stick.

1 Stand the cardboard box upright on the table, with the opening toward you. Work 'inside' the box, as shown, in order to protect your work area. Place a sheet of paper inside the box, and arrange a few leaves on the paper. Dab the brush with paint. Splatter the paint around the leaves by gently drawing the stick toward you across the bristles of the brush.

2 The finished effect.

3 *An Autumn Leaf*

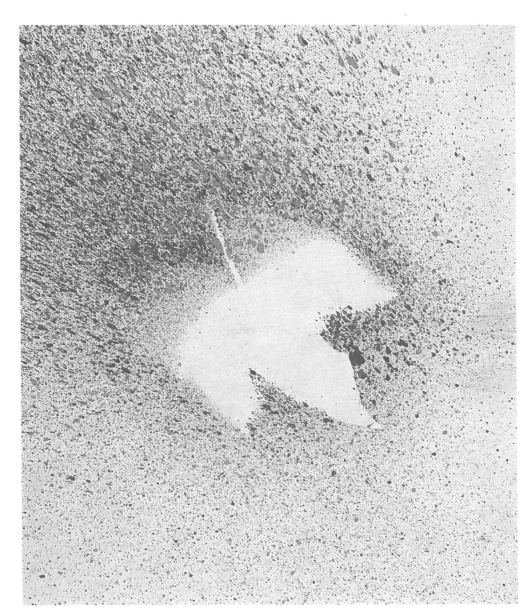

Sprayed decorative papers

A second way of splattering color is by diffusion.

You will need paper, a diffuser spray, colored inks, and an iron. You will also need to cover your work table and any nearby walls or furniture with old newspaper, for protection.

4 Crumple a piece of paper, then open it out so that the creases are still bumpy. Use the diffuser to spray ink across the paper.

The ink will cover the surfaces that face you but will not touch the areas that face away from you.

5 Turn the paper around and spray again, using a second color.

6 Let the paper dry, then iron it.

7 *Mystical Mountains.* An ironed sprayed paper using just one color.

8 Try this method of splattering color again. This time fold a piece of paper, accordion style. Open the paper out, so that the accordion folds stand up. Spray ink across the folds . . .

9 . . . then turn the paper around so that the opposite sides of the folds face you. Spray again, using a second color.

10 The finished paper, ironed. The sprayed ink makes the paper seem as if it is still folded.

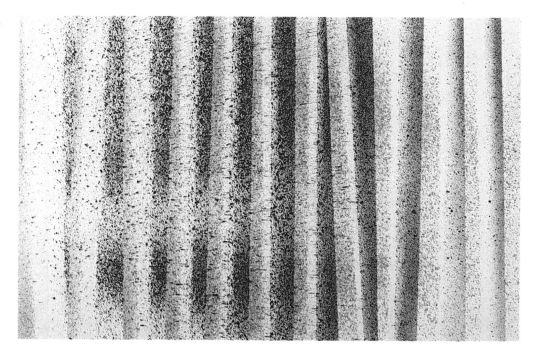

11 Sprayed paper that was folded in a fan shape.

12 A small gift wrapped as a cracker, with a matching card. To make the card, cut a strip from the sprayed paper, fold it into an accordion, and glue it to the front of the card so the the folds stand out and create a 3-D effect.

Screen-printed papers

Screen-printing is another way of decorating papers using a stencil. Ink is forced through a fabric screen, and a colored print is made around the stencil design.

You will need a pencil, paper, scissors, a screen-printing frame and squeegee, and water-based printing inks.

1 Draw a design on a sheet of paper. Here a symmetrical design is being made on folded paper.

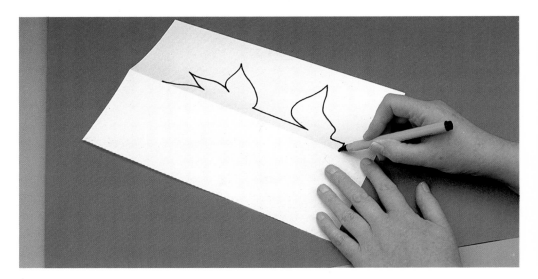

2 Cut out the design. This cutout shape is your stencil.

3 Lay the stencil on top of the sheet of paper that is to be printed, and place the screen on top.

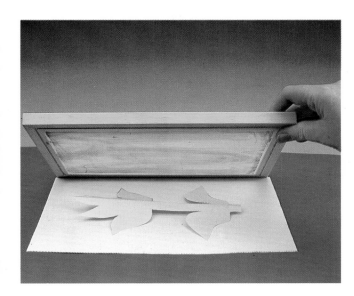

4 Squeeze some ink along one edge of the screen. Press the squeegee firmly against the screen and pull it across, taking the color with it.

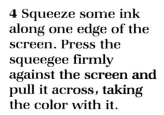

5 Lift the screen to reveal the print. The area without color is in the shape of the stencil.

6 A selection of screen prints. The print on the bottom right was made by using the cutout design *(top right)* as the stencil.

7 To make a two-color print, wash the screen with water and prepare a second stencil by cutting away more shapes from the basic design. Allow the first color to dry before applying the second color over the original print.

8 A finished two-color print.

Decorating papers with a sponge printing block is easy and fun.

You will need pieces of sponge, scissors, cardboard, glue, paints, paper and glitter.

1 Experiment first with a small piece of sponge. Print with each of the sponge's edges in turn. Do the results you achieve vary? Try curling one of the edges to obtain a curved pattern.

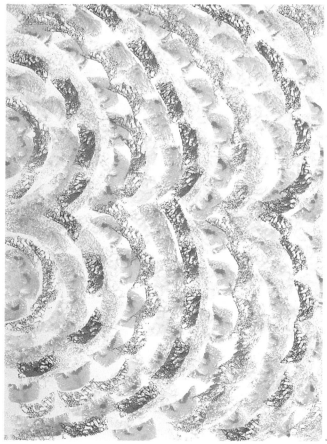

2 A sponge-printed design.

3 Another colorful pattern.

4 Cut some shapes from the pieces of sponge. Glue each shape onto a piece of cardboard. Set aside to dry. These are your printing blocks.

5 Dip the sponge shapes in paint, and print onto a sheet of paper. Using very little paint gives a pleasing, mottled effect.

6 Try adding glitter to your decorated paper while the paint is still wet.

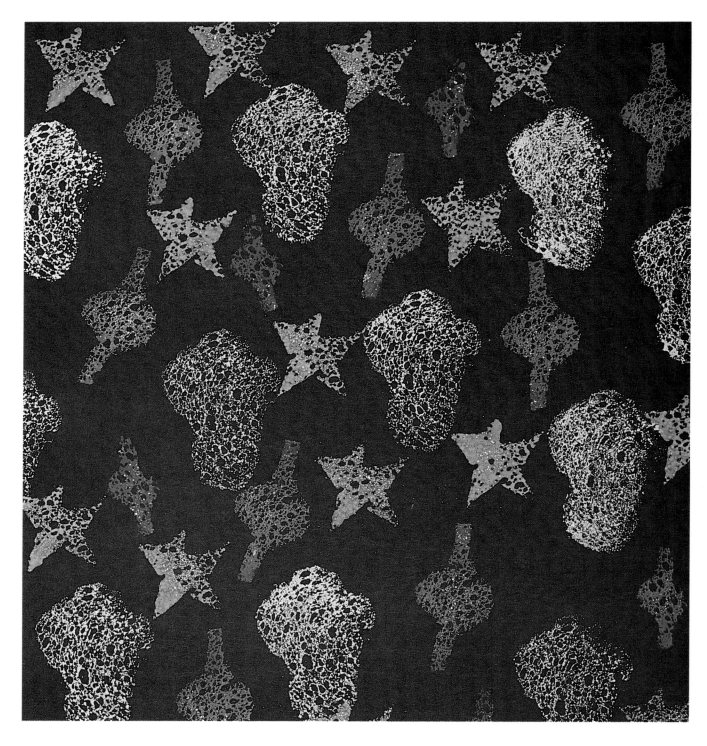

7 *Clouds, Stars and Planets.* The finished paper.

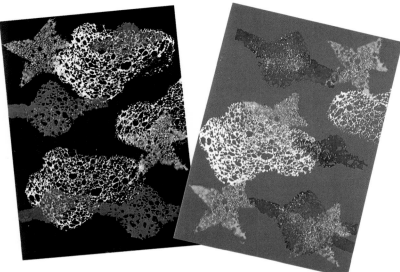

8 Make greeting cards using the same method. Try printing on different colored papers.

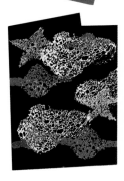

9 An individually printed paper makes a lovely surprise for your friends and relatives.

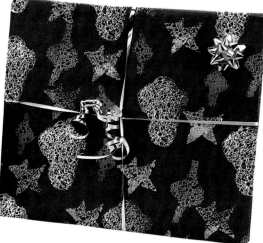

10 Use a sponge block to print a set of small cards. Use these as gift tags or as place settings at a party.

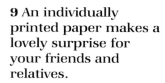

Marbling inks are oil-based colors and are often used in the art of decorative paper making.

You will need a tray of water, marbling inks, a thin stick, sheets of paper, and wallpaper paste.

1 Drip a few spots of marbling color onto the surface of the water. With the tip of the stick, gently swirl the colors into a pattern.

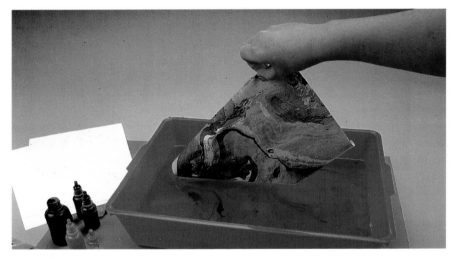

2 Lay a sheet of paper over the water, then lift it out carefully. Set aside to dry.

3 If you wish to control the spread of colors in your pattern, add some wallpaper paste to the water. Allow it to thicken (it should be the consistency of thin cream), then drip some drops of marbling color onto the surface of the paste.

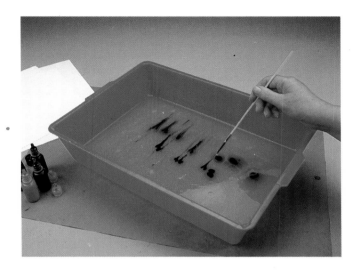

4 Pull the tip of the
stick across the colors,
first in one direction…

5 … then in the other
direction.

6 Lay a sheet of paper
over the surface …

7 … then lift the
paper.

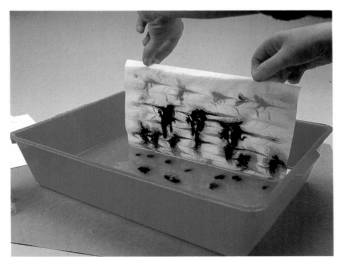

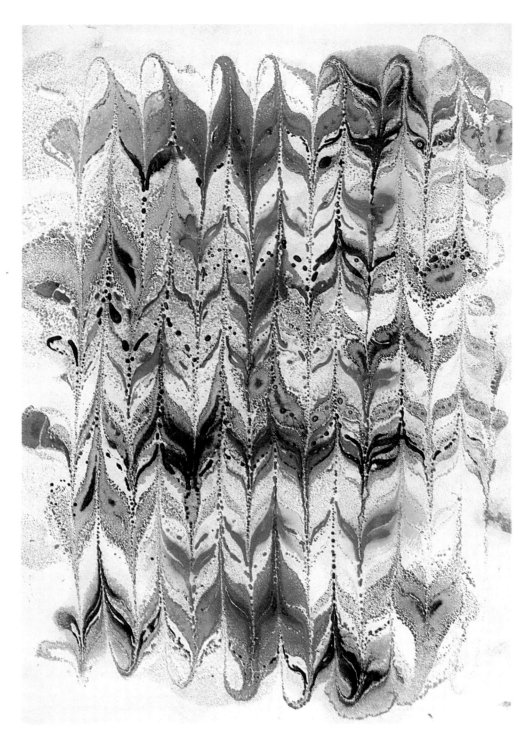

8 A feathered design. The wallpaper paste prevents the colors from spreading.

9 Experiment with different colors to produce your own marbled design.

10 A small box covered with marbled paper makes an attractive container for a small gift. Make a greeting card to accompany your gift by mounting a section of your marbled paper on to a piece of thin cardboard.

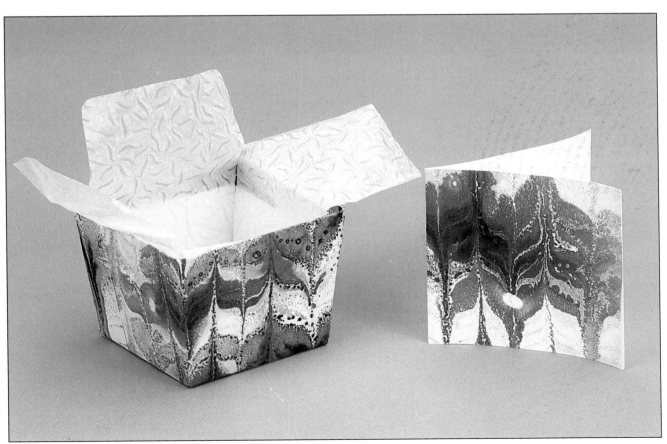

Attractive decorated papers can be made by folding and dyeing. In this way, plain white paper napkins or paper towels can be transformed into colorful party table napkins!

You will need paper napkins or paper towels, and a selection of different colored inks or cold-water dyes.

1 Prepare your napkins or paper towels by folding them in different ways – into squares or triangles, for example, or by twisting, rolling or pleating. Dip one end of a folded paper into the ink or dye, then lift it out quickly so that only a little color is absorbed. Repeat by dipping the other end of the paper, then the middle.

2 Allow to dry, then unfold gently.

3 An attractive place setting for a party. As well as being arranged decoratively in the glasses, the patterned napkins can also be used as placemats.

4 Notice the sponge-printed place setting cards and the gifts wrapped in home-made decorated paper. Happy birthday!

Here are a few more activities for
you to try.

A decorated paper book cover

1 Use decorated
papers to make a
cover for a book or
folder. Use two sheets
of thick cardboard and
cover them carefully
with two of your
decorated sheets.
Punch two holes at
one end of each cover
and make a string tie
to hold the pages.

Your own notepaper

2 Prepare a tray of
marbling color. Dip
one edge of a sheet of
paper into the water
and lift it out. The
marbling color will
make an attractive
border on both sides
of your notepaper.

3 Repeat for the other
three edges.

4 You can make a set of matching notepaper by using the same tray of ink.

An envelope for a greeting card or sheet of notepaper

5 Select a sheet of decorated paper. Here, a sheet of marbled paper has been chosen. Fold and cut an envelope to fit your greeting card or notepaper, as shown. Make the envelope slightly larger than the card so that the card will slip in and out easily.

6 You may wish to have the marbled pattern on the inside of your envelope.

7 Fold the bottom flap up, and glue it to the side flaps of the envelope. Use a white gummed label for the name if necessary.

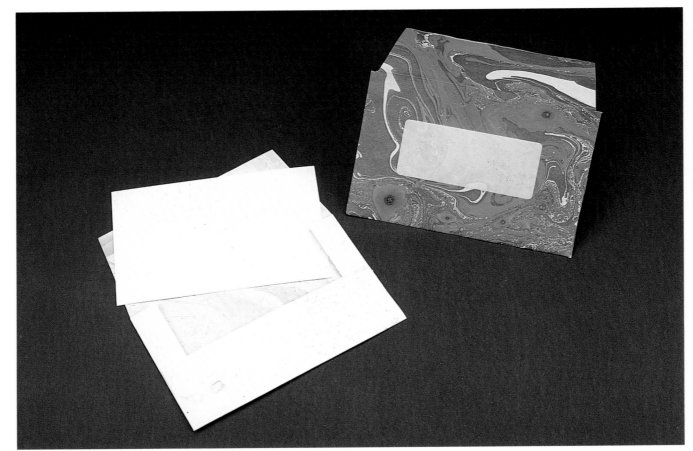

Most of the materials mentioned in this book are easy to obtain.

Paper and card
Most stationers stock a good range of paper and cardboard in different weights and colors.

Printing inks
Some recommended water-based inks are: Grumbacher and Berol.

Printing rollers
These are obtainable in a variety of widths. A width of 4in is an average size and is recommended for the activities in this book.

Special materials
Special materials such as marbling inks, boiled linseed oil and printing rollers can be obtained from art supply and craft stores.

Scoring cardboard
If you want to fold a piece of cardboard so that the folded edge is straight and neat, you should "score" the cardboard first. Place the piece of cardboard flat on a cutting board, and position a metal ruler on the cardboard so that one of its long edges follows exactly the line of the fold you want to make. Hold a craft knife in your "work" hand, blade pointing downward, and hold the ruler down firmly with your other hand. Run the craft knife firmly down the edge of the metal ruler which lies along the fold line, cutting *into* the cardboard as you do so but not cutting *through* it. Once a piece of cardboard has been scored in this way, you will find it easier to fold the cardboard in the way you want.